WALK LIKE
THE BIRD FLIES

poems by

Susan Ayres

Finishing Line Press
Georgetown, Kentucky

WALK LIKE
THE BIRD FLIES

ACKNOWLEDGMENTS

Grateful acknowledgement is made to the editors of the following
publications, in which these poems first appeared:

Broadkill Review: "The Gray Lady," "Town Beach, Split," "Foreign Cities, 1,"
"Foreign Cities, 2," "Foreign Cities, 3," "Foreign Cities, 4"
Concho River Review: "Port Aransas Vigil"
descant: "Pecos Cantaloupes"
Eunoia Review: "Rain in the Green Mountains," "On the Talala Trail, Cedar
Hill State Park," "Taqueria Molina"
Main Street Rag: "The Capuchin Bridge"
Neologism Poetry Journal: "Wildfire"
Rat's Ass Review: "Painting of the Red Bridge"
Rogue Agent: "Sacred Breasts"
Southwest Review: "Most People Die Unevolved"
Willows Wept Review: "Trouvelot's Crater"

Publisher: Leah Huete de Maines
Editor: Christen Kincaid
Cover Art: Scott Lennox
Author Photo: Allyson Wolfe
Cover Design: Elizabeth Maines McCleavy

Order online: www.finishinglinepress.com
also available on amazon.com

Author inquiries and mail orders:
Finishing Line Press
PO Box 1626
Georgetown, Kentucky 40324
USA

Table of Contents

For David
and for Daniel, Katie, and Ben

traveler, there is no road,
the road is made by walking
                    —Antonio Machado

RAIN IN THE GREEN MOUNTAINS

after Octavio Paz

Listen to me as one listens to the rain
hitting the leaves silently
while crows caw somewhere
in the glistening maple canopy

and wild strawberries ripen
each day. Is that what the bear
searched for last night? I didn't
see it in the darkness, but heard

it crashing through bushes. Listen to me
as one listens to the rain
falling in sheets against lightning
and the dark sky. The woods are hidden
and everything is silent now except

the storm. The cows kneel
their shaggy red coats until dawn. Paths
have filled with rivulets. I stand
by the window and hear

you light a fire. Rivers
swell to overflowing, ponds
appear in ditches, thorny blackberry
brambles invade gardens. This week

we spend in the mountains, content
to walk along ferns and horsetail
to the small stone chapel where
we pull the rope to ring the bell
announcing our presence like

that of the bear, like the raindrops
that bounce off the wooden
steps, slide down birch leaves, tickle
the lime-green edges of the larch.

THE GRAY LADY

The tide up, she took a curve too fast, drove into the Atlantic. As we drifted out, she said, "This is no good," so there was nothing to do but swim out the windows and watch the car catch the Gulf Stream to California. My job was to pick up broken glass reflecting sunlight on the Nantucket beach like it was my fault. I wasn't even driving, but there is no accounting for guilt these days. Later, drinking chardonnay by the blue and pink hydrangeas, we agreed it was an accident. We were close to disaster, but swam out the windows. With no other clothes, no shoes, we knew we had nothing to lose, so in town we bought black linen dresses and shot photos against the pink and orange sunset. It was the day Princess Di died, our hems dripping wet, the fog rolling in.

PAINTING OF THE RED BRIDGE

> *The color of truth is gray.*
> *—Andre Gide*

The red bridge squats
eponymously over blue water.
Demolished years before the artist's

birth, the red bridge is painted
from imagination, painted from directions
given over generations: *Take the Red Bridge . . .*

In a place where things don't change
much, where grandparents may never
have travelled out of the state, much less

the country, the red bridge has been
reconstructed since slavery. Unlike
the lead-colored smokestacks lurching

into sight as I-95 curves into town, the red
bridge sits not in a place, but in collective
memory, joining Providence to East

Providence. How do you get there? You
take the red bridge. Today's bridge is no
longer red, but everyone knows what you mean.

The color of truth is gray, like
smokestacks. The color of nostalgia
is heart-hued. My bridge flies cochineal across

the Seekonk River, your bridge hovers
rust-red like an abandoned train trestle. This
painted bridge squats carmine. Everyone knows
you eat raw oysters in months that have an *r* in them.

PECOS CANTALOUPES

Halfway across Texas
we'd stop every summer in Pecos
for cantaloupes by the bag full.
My father would deliver us
to my grandmother
and after a day or two,
he'd head back west.
My mother and sister and I would enjoy
a month or more at Lake Buchanan.

Our days passed slowly and sweetly
as the cantaloupes ripened.
Every day my grandmother sewed
dresses, coats, and shirts for the school year,
and we patiently stopped our play to stand still
for hems to be pinned, sleeves measured.
My mother did all the finishing by hand
while my sister and I swam
or rode bikes or fed birds.
We picked wildflowers—
brown-eyed Susans, Mexican hats—
and collected shells or driftwood.
And every night we left the dinner dishes
in the sink for the morning.
And every night we watched the 8 o'clock
movie and ate a cantaloupe half
filled with Gandy's vanilla ice cream.

The cantaloupes were real Pecos cantaloupes.
They were small, maybe five inches
in diameter, and sweet.
Perfect ice cream bowls,
not like the ones you buy today.
I could be wrong,
but in my memory, the days
and weeks and summers themselves
were as sweet and ripe
and irreplaceable as clothes sewn
by hand and bags full of Pecos cantaloupes.

MOST PEOPLE DIE UNEVOLVED

Thou shouldst not have been old till
thou hadst been wise.
                    —King Lear

It's been three months. Mother buried,
I call my father, and mention my trip
to Langtry, Texas. How Judge Roy Bean—
one of his heroes—served there as justice of the peace.
Dad cuts me off.
"I know Judge Roy Bean was never in Langtry.

Whatever you think is wrong
and I don't want to hear
anything else about Langtry."

I think, *drinking*. But my husband
says, "Most people die unevolved," meaning
my father's just a character like Judge Roy Bean

living in Eagle's Nest, later called Langtry,
across the Rio Grande from Mexico
where a pair of eagles roosted

far above the river in a limestone overhang.
You can still see the nest today
in that town of falling wooden structures.

Back then it was busy with railroad workers,
Texas Rangers, soldiers, and women
of ill repute. In the 1880s Bean opened

a saloon— The Jersey Lilly—after the English actress
he worshipped, Lillie Langtry.
The saloon was also the courtroom.

Jurors were bar patrons
who bought drinks when court recessed.
They tried horse thieves and murderers.

Bean was called the hanging judge,
the Law West of the Pecos
even though he decided it was no crime

to kill a Chinaman.
Even though Bean assaulted
his wife who bore four children

and went back to Mexico. His children later left
on the railroad that went through
Langtry then. It skirted sheer cliffs

above the Pecos River.
People watched for rattlesnakes,
scorpions, prickly pears, the Milky Way.

People traveled miles
when prizefights were illegal
to watch a fight Bean organized.

It lasted a minute-and-a-half
before knock-out
in a dried riverbed neither Texas nor Mexico.

In 1903 Judge Roy Bean drank
himself to death people said,
and like most who die,

Bean wasn't evolved.
But he was a picaro, an original.
Born in Kentucky in 1825,

he began evading justice in Mexico,
San Diego, Los Angeles, New Mexico,
San Antonio, and various small

settlements in west Texas
where the Pecos River
and the Rio Grande meet,

where Lillie Langtry
visited ten months too late
to claim his heart.

What part of this story do you want
to deny most, Dad—the drink,
the outlaw justice, the unclaimed heart?

PORT ARANSAS VIGIL

We felt guilty having any fun
while Cindy was dying hundreds of miles away.
Every several hours, you checked in,
cried at reports of her suffering.
One time, her son answered, *Pete's Pizza Parlor.*
You thought his levity inappropriate.
Maybe it was desire for anything besides
her slow dying,
besides steady calls from friends
needing and giving consolation.
We walked to the pier
past the aluminum trailer,
past the brown condo high-rise,
not to wait
but to watch dolphins leaping at dusk.

ON THE TALALA TRAIL, CEDAR HILL STATE PARK

Talala is Cherokee for woodpecker

The muddy clay grass weeds stuck to the bottom of my sneakers like what's caking my soul bogged down with mud and clay and straw, my airy soul, anima alma animus of my dreamworld between the worlds weighted with claymud tromping a path I choose, in the drizzle always that claymud as I drag my feet over the grass trying to clean some of it off, trying to keep my soul clean, free of all that muddy mess of a path that's under construction, which means re-tracing my steps instead of going on, re-tracing what isn't my soul-work, how easily I get bogged down, mired in it, losing my way until I reach the overlook foggy drizzle everything gray, there's no lake, no horizon, no lookout but vast emptiness like the Gulf, the yawning void, the hills a mirage in the place the horizon should be, late afternoon gray, deathlike calm punctuated by crow caws, no woodpeckers or hawks, silence and the way out and past where a boat carries the soul to the other side and those souls busy themselves watching us bog ourselves down, watch us making choices as if we had no choice on such a gray, drizzly day, but to cake our souls in mudclay.

WILDFIRE

after Lorca

Where is my old voice
       dripping dew from spiked
              maples onto my hands?

My liquid voice almost a whisper.
       My voice when I was solid and
              certain, before I quavered like a charred

aspen whistling beneath the moon.
       My voice when I was a ragged
              ponderosa, bark-bruised by antlers.

Ten years later, landscape
       still ravaged. Charred hollow trunks
              scattered over mountains. I want

my old voice, chirping like wrens
       in silver-gray branches. I want
              your touch without your destruction.

EL DIABLO ON INTERSTATE 10

In the distance we saw it—
dirt swirling faster
column rising taller.
As my son and I sped west

it rushed east, parallel
to the road. Who can say
if it was spinning clockwise
or counterclockwise? Off in the south
you could see rain
falling in Mexico, where people
make the sign of the cross
when they see *el diablo.*

Some call them *remolinos,*
twisters. Some say
they don't signify anything at all.
I have always loved spotting
dirt devils, usually in the distance,
in an otherwise still landscape,
brief dance of dust
and wind reaching up to the sky.

The temperature gauge
read 104, the posted speed limit
85, a landscape of mountains,
mesquite, yucca—not unlike
our trip to Greece when I convinced
Daniel to re-enact Orestes' flight
out of Mycenae. Now, he lives
hundreds of miles away,

out of my orbit of protection,
now I try to keep my eyes on the road,
but I've never seen
a dirt devil this close, dancing
up the highway's shoulder, until
it sideswipes his window and door—
a rain of dirt and rocks,
a sudden shower tagging him.

What does it portend?
Message from beyond
or mere coincidence,
El diablo's grasp
or nature's ecstatic dance?

TACQUERIA MOLINA

There was the chef's hand.
He squeezed the *cochinita pibil*
and shredded it with his hands.

All the bones fell to the ground.
Afterwards the smells swirled
around guides leading green-vested

tourists through stalls
past plastic bags of bones and fat
past plucked chickens

with toenails splayed in the air
past iced fish and a little girl twirling.
The bones of my heart

swirled, chile burned my lips
as I watched a seamstress
patch a pirate's sail to withstand

the north wind under a black
sky and hidden moon.

TOWN BEACH, SPLIT

The teething baby eats rocks. Her mother scolds,
"Ne, ne, ne." The teething baby's name
is Lela. Crowded on the beach, sunbathing women,

with power to caress a scraped knee or warm thigh,
lead a lover to bed by the hand. Here by the sea
everyone smiles at children running and screaming

into the cold Adriatic. People eat apricots and leave
pits in the sand. The huge red billboard is for the local
beer, *Karlovačko*, bottle crowned like a king. *Spasilac*

says the lifeguard's chair, and I think "spastic," like baby
Lela choking on rocks her mother tries to dig out of her mouth.
The Croatian all around me is white noise

like the waves and screams and pebbly sand. Universal
language is touch and baby talk. Lela's mother
says "Yummy," and hands Lela a teething biscuit. Couples

stroll up and down the shore holding hands. Bars play
rock and roll. I order a cappuccino, distracted by English
lyrics that drag my thoughts up the stairway of Led

Zeppelin and dump me in the sea. I sink to the bottom
where sardele caress the nape of my neck, the small
of my back, nibble my ears like a lover I've forgotten,

children I've left behind, grape seeds I've buried in the sand.

LJUBLJANA MUSIC FESTIVAL

A puff of cottony plant rises in the breeze
and English ivy sways over the marble terrace
of this medieval fortress
                    where it's hot and still
under the huge canvas umbrella shading
my table against the afternoon sun.
Sweat runs down my back.

I'm trying to carry less. My umbrella
and wallet left behind. The lightest
linen and cotton on my body.
I want to be transparent and light
like the few coins and bills I carry
in a Ziploc bag. The one card
that can be used for identification.

                    Tonight when I leave
the piano concerto, I will want to fly.
I will want to live with the blood
and duende of those great pianists
                    who play like children.

Like Martha Agerich, who will laugh
tonight when she slams
her hands down on the keys to stop
the trumpeter in the last
movement of Shostakovich. And José Feghali.
Whenever I watched him play
he beamed over the piano, eyes closed,
body swaying to the rhythm his hands found.

                    Martha will play like a child
but walk with the hips
of an old woman. José is gone, so young.

The *duende* is light.
How close to death
must one be to feel it?

THE CAPUCHIN BRIDGE

Here in the red-tiled village
of Škofja Loka, I cross the 14th century
stone bridge Bishop Leopold built.
The story's told he fell off his horse

and drowned. Outside my window,
cathedral bells ring all day. A bronze
Saint John of Nepomuk raises a hand
in blessing. His mitered head bends

to a crucifix, and five stars dance
round his brow. The story's told
he drowned, in a river to the north,
now in Prague. Some say he refused

to betray the queen's confession—
lovers she named. Look up. Tonight
clouds hide starlight. All night, rain
fills the river. Who would have seen

the five stars that rose from the drowned body,
heard cries from the dungeon, iron tools
used to coerce names from the pierced
tongue? Rain doesn't wet my tongue's

truth of dreams. Thunder doesn't break
my sleep. Starshine marked the spot his body
was thrown in the river and found. I confess
my sins to no one, eat apricots, cherries,

drink the red Teran wine. Later I'll stand
by the bridge's iron rail, spit pits into the muddy
river as it rushes downstream into history.

THE CLASSICAL DEBT

we will never repay the debt we owe Greece
            —Stephen Fry, Elgin Marbles Debate

1.

Greek waiters talk not
        to me, but my son. Hotel
                staff tells me it's unseemly

for women to travel
        alone. Mornings, I take
                my coffee to Athens' National

Park, where a monkey
        bit King Alexander
                and he died. I do not feel

safe here, do not walk
        alone at night, not even
                in the touristy Plaka

past sleeping men under
        eaves of shops that once
                sold olive oil, leather sandals,

Byzantine icons, replica gods.
        She's gone too—Athena, fierce
                warrior with her fierce gray stare.

2.

When I was a girl in El Paso,
        our Greek friend refused
                to give away

his daughter in marriage.
      She had dishonored him—
            Catholic girls got pregnant

since birth control was
      a sin. Apparently
            forgivable, since Father Finnegan

let one girl play
      "Having My Baby" during
            her wedding mass. Visiting

Greece is a throwback
      to my girlhood of mighty
            Church, mighty Father, Aegean

blue like the Virgin's
      robes, where my son refuses
            to swim.

      3.

The bread is delivered
      without your asking. The best
            comes with olives, hummus,

beet dip. The appetizer
      not ordered is included
            in the bill, as if the debt

we owe Greece will be paid
      bite-by-bite. We are responsible
            for the country's bankruptcy, for

its small pipes we clog
     with toilet paper, for its graffiti,
          its unemployed. We pay for bottled

water when the server claims
     there is no tap water.
          This country feels more oriental

than occidental, my son
     comments. And I see
          what he means. It's

as if we descended directly
     from Lord Elgin or stole
          the marbles ourselves. It's

as if bread, water, toilets will
     be bartered in this cradle
          of civilization

where we owe, owe, owe.

SACRED BREASTS

Naturally, I was sick at the Asclepion. The late afternoon heat, the double cappuccino fredo on the curvy road from Naufplio to Epidaurus. The sun, the dust. The lost lover, the failing marriage. I wandered nauseous through crumbling foundations of the Great Stoa, the Temple, the Banqueting Hall, broken columns, weeds. Inside the stifling museum, a wall of clay votives, offerings of thanks for healing dreams: ears, arms, legs, eyes, breasts, heads, kidneys. The gallery floor filled with sculptures. An Artemis torso covered with dangling breasts, Asclepius with a snake. Two fans blew hot air. I prayed to the headless statute of Hygeia, daughter of Asclepius. The moon was full, the ancient seats were hard. I sipped Sparky and watched Medea lose her husband, her mind. Regret also waited back in the States. Purged of hope, my nights remain dreamless. No god or goddess offers me a cure.

FOREIGN CITIES, 1

Outside Vera, groves of olive trees dot a landscape dusty and otherwise barren. The bus that takes you into the heart of the city is an accordion bus with announcements made in an unpardonable tongue. The city has layers of history, but someone had to choose which layer to display. The sidewalks have random slabs of glass you can peer through to see excavated buildings from 100 B.C. You feel unsteady walking on glass sidewalks. In cathedrals, the devout kiss the icons of saints, leaving lip smudges on the framed glass. In cafés, wine is cheaper than water but you can dine with the ancient columns in view. The history that is told is more Judeo-Christian than Asian. There are more archaic torsos than pickpockets, more taxis than painted vases. The stream where the North Wind raped a river nymph lies buried under the orange line.

FOREIGN CITIES, 2

Sometimes when you are travelling and have that sense that you've forgotten something, it's nothing. Other times, it's your wallet on the train, your jacket on the bed, your power charger in the outlet. Your name, your heart. The heart that tries to forget. The calming heartbeat. The eyes of St. Cecilia—blue disks on a white plate. Sunglasses and umbrellas left behind at the beach bar of Dara, a tiny town. The whole point of visiting is the sea. Sunbathing and swimming in the sea. The beach is silky smooth and pleasant to walk on in the morning before the sun bakes the sand. In the nearby taberna, you eat moussaka, pastitsio, and the owner's big white rabbit hops under tables when she's not in the shopping cart parked next to the entrance. Everyone tries to take a photo with the fluffy bunny. Meals last three hours and end with a sweet dessert wine, some fruit. As you stroll back to the beach, you have that sensation you've left something behind. Your beach hat, which you must walk back and retrieve. And more importantly, you've forgotten the clock, keys, jewels of blood. You're as empty as the waves that will lull you to sleep.

FOREIGN CITIES, 3

When you arrive in Anya, cobblestone streets wind around shops and taverns inside the medieval walls. No cars are allowed. The moat has been dry thousands of years. It was never filled with water. Like other port towns, cats slink under tavern chairs, waiting for scraps of overpriced seafood. The pistachio gelato always sells out. The melody from *Zorba* can be heard into the wee hours when men link arms to dance near the lighthouse and old men and women sit outside open doors, loudly debating who should be the next saint. Artists have painted a mural on Town Hall depicting the bloodiest battles. Over three hundred pirates have been executed, but the seas still crawl with them. The town pretends the problem is under control, but in fact it's an illusion. The whole town is a permanent movie set, an illusion. *Zorba* is filmed day-in and day-out. If you visit, you can sign up to be an extra, can watch the sand waves galloping on fire in the sunlight. Mesmerizing gray-green-blue of stirred up sand, and the aqua blue past the buoys marking the swim area. Dark steel blue out to sky where there seems to be a line of light gray on the horizon. If there's such a thing as horizon between water and sky.

FOREIGN CITIES, 4

A young boy walks by pressing his shirt over his nose while adults ignore the stench hovering over the barely moving urban river, packed with tourists, conventioneers. The stench of river and restaurant clean-outs oppresses in Santiago's afternoon heat. The smell masked by the steak house and the café's tortillas and beans. The sense of smell dulled by margaritas and beer. Even the bright orange pomegranate pompoms are wilting. Homeless people hold signs. "Anything Appreciated." One man randomly shouts out curses. "Fuck you, bitch." You do not take it personally. Posters advertise a jazz festival at a nearby park. You consider walking over, but remain alone in the cold, dark room overlooking tall palms. Named after a saint, the city is less heaven than purgatory. The Spanish missions long abandoned, the city's gods are the tall basketball players covered in tattoos. Buildings have been re-purposed, the brewery now a museum, the quarry now a shopping mall. The military commands a presence. You are awakened by reveille and cannot remember what you dreamed or what drew you to visit.

TROUVELOT'S CRATER

> *We especially need imagination in science. It is not all*
> *mathematics, nor all logic, but . . . beauty and poetry.*
> —Maria Mitchell

> *No human skill can reproduce . . . the majestic beauty and*
> *radiance of the celestial objects.*
> —Étienne Trouvelot

I. Little Egg

Gypsy moth
Shaping the future.
Wild wanderer
White winged with brown chevrons
You lay eggs on oak, maple, birch,
Spruce—on lawn chairs and trucks.
Your egg-mass like millions
Before you

∧ ∧ ∧ ∧ ∧   ∧ ∧ ∧ ∧   ∧ ∧ ∧ ∧   ∧ ∧ ∧ ∧   ∧ ∧ ∧ ∧

II. Munching

Dangling from threads
Lifted downwind to host
Trees, holy leaves.
Holy crash of continents
Hundreds of millions of years since
These Green Mountains formed.
Dark brown caterpillars.

The busy sound of actually.
To my desert eye everything is green.
I listen closer:
The sound of caterpillars
Munching leaves, dropping waste
A noise like raindrops dropping.
Crimson and indigo dots cover their abdomens.

They pluck 350,000 acres in Massachusetts alone.
Busier than our great grandmothers plucking
Hens for Sunday dinner, soldiers plucking buffalo
Near extinction to solve "The Indian Problem."

∧ ∧ ∧ ∧ ∧   ∧ ∧ ∧ ∧   ∧ ∧ ∧ ∧   ∧ ∧ ∧ ∧   ∧ ∧ ∧ ∧

III. Hatching

Rain feeds the Japanese fungus
That kills the caterpillars.
Entomophaga maimaiga
Kills gypsy moths, not blue swallowtails,

Monarchs, silkworms, or anything else.
Without rain, the fungus dries, the caterpillars
Grow. How did the fungus get here? No one knows.

> *The gypsy moth . . . an extreme example of an introduced*
> *organism exploding*
> *out of control throughout an alien ecosystem.*

Invasive exotics: knotweed, garlic mustard,
Dutch Elm disease, Chestnut blight. Gypsy
Moths. Unfortunate for us,
No natural predators.

Honeybees in white clover.
August insects swarming. The small brown
Males mate with larger flightless
Females. Eggs hatch early spring, and by July
I sneeze at blooming goldenrod
& caterpillars whose barbed hairs
Repel birds, beetles, mice, squirrels, foxes.

Grackles have been observed in Armstrong County, PA,
beating gypsy moth larvae repeatedly across the rough
surface of an asphalt street, thus removing the hairs
before ingesting the larvae.

You might think
The leafless maples and oaks, the naked spruces
And cedars a result of illness or
Drought or lightning strike
Or just bad soil.
You might not notice bare trees,
Limbs in the verdant mountains
Of New England, my friend's
Stripped crepe myrtle in Texas, an entire
Apricot orchard in British Columbia.

PRESS RELEASE April 20, 1947:

The U.S. Department of Agriculture this year
starts its annual campaign against the gypsy
moth with higher hopes than ever before for the
eventual eradication of this destructive insect
pest. . . .DDT, it was found, kills every young
gypsy moth caterpillar coming in contact with
it. . . . Airplanes fitted with various devices
throw out a highly concentrated DDT solution as
a very fine mist over a 100-foot swath at the
rate of 3 acres every 3 minutes.

Abenaki in Vermont. Japanese in WW II. Buffalo. Today
"invasive exotics" cross our southern border. Our mistakes multiply.

The question is whether any civilization can wage
relentless war on life without destroying itself &
without losing the right to be called civilized.

Scientists hope
The "final solution"
To gypsy moths will be the Japanese fungus

Or pheromones to trick the males.

∧ ∧ ∧ ∧ ∧   ∧ ∧ ∧ ∧   ∧ ∧ ∧ ∧   ∧ ∧ ∧ ∧   ∧ ∧ ∧ ∧

IV. Soaring

During Napoleon III's coup d'état,
Étienne Léopold Trouvelot fled to America, 1855.

Occupation: lithographer
Avocation: scientist
Experiment: hybridize silkworms with gypsy moths for disease-
resistant worms
(Cotton shortage, Civil War)
Method: clear US customs with French gypsy moths, 1867

Several years later, a storm or curious child broke
The netting on his backyard insectary at 27 Myrtle Street
Medford, Mass. A decade later, neighbors'
Trees ravaged, vegetable gardens as well. He searched
For escapees, notified authorities
But the pestilence spread—Massachusetts

To Rhode Island, Connecticut, New York,
Pennsylvania, Maryland, Oregon, North Carolina,
Michigan, sea to shining sea.

Conifers will die after only one heavy defoliation event
Hardwoods might survive a season or two.

∧ ∧ ∧ ∧ ∧   ∧ ∧ ∧ ∧   ∧ ∧ ∧ ∧   ∧ ∧ ∧ ∧   ∧ ∧ ∧ ∧

V. Sketching

Trouvelot turned from silkworms to
Skies, drawing celestial bodies
Through the biggest telescopes of the time:
Harvard, U.S. Naval Observatory.

Some of his 7,000 celestial pastels
Displayed at the 1876 World Fair, along with Bell's
First telephone, Heinz Ketchup, and the right
Arm of the Statute of Liberty.

The Trouvelot Astronomical Drawings Manual (1882):
200 pages of text &
15 chromolithographs 28 x 32 inches.
The drawing of Mars is
An orange and black cat's eye
Marble against a black field. Sunspots are
Dancing hydras or dandelions blown
Inside-out. A hundred years later, a folio
Sold for $60,000.

Trouvelot: "the prince of observers"
Of planets, Sun, comets, Mars,
Saturn, Jupiter, Moon, meteors, nebulas,
Aurora Borealis, bodies we've named
Milky Way, zodiacal light.
Just as we named a lunar crater "Trouvelot"
Gypsy moths already had a name—
Porthetria dispar in his time, *Lymantria dispar* now.

Devoted "prince of observers," dead in France, 1895. Most
Of the pastels lost, color plates lost. So many hours
Gazing into *the starry vault*, the light of *our nearest celestial
neighbor*, the Moon—

Who taught you to sketch?
Did you dream in color?
Teach your children the constellations?
Imagine life in *the immense belt of soft white light*
    called the Milky Way?
Did you love your wife more than *the majestic beauty and radiance*
    of the celestial objects?

With their *pale, glimmering luminosity*
similar to peach blossoms . . . delicate prismatic hues . . . pink and straw
Saturn, the most beautiful and interesting of all . . .

∧ ∧ ∧ ∧   ∧ ∧ ∧ ∧   ∧ ∧ ∧ ∧   ∧ ∧ ∧ ∧   ∧ ∧ ∧ ∧

NOTES

"The Gray Lady": Nantucket was often shrouded in fog, so sailors called her *The Gray Lady*.

"Trouvelot's Crater": The italicized phrase in Part II is from *Cascadia* by Brenda Hillman. Part III quotes scientists' reports on gypsy moths and a sentence from Rachel Carson's *Silent Spring*. Part IV quotes a fact sheet from the Mass. Dept. of Conservation & Recreation. Part V quotes articles about Trouvelot's drawings and information from *The Trouvelot Astronomical Drawings Manual*.

Susan Ayres is a poet, lawyer, and translator. She holds an MFA in creative writing from Vermont College of Fine Arts, a PhD in literature from Texas Christian University, and a JD from Baylor University. Her work has been nominated for a Pushcart Prize, and has appeared in dozens of journals, including *Louisville Review, South Carolina Review, Sycamore Review, Cimarron Review, Ilanot Review,* and *Valparaiso Review.*

Her translations from the Spanish include the work of Mexican poets Elsa Cross, David Anuar, and Adriana Cupul Itzá, as well as Peruvian fiction writers Dany Salvatierra, Romina Paredes, Maria José Caro, and Tadeo Palacios. She has served as translator for *The South Carolina Review*'s Latin American Series, guest translation co-editor for *The Loch Raven Review*, and reader for *Hunger Mountain Review* and Perugia Press.

Ayres was raised in the desert of west Texas and grew up surrounded by the Franklin Mountains. She now lives in Fort Worth with her husband, and teaches at Texas A&M University School of Law, where she publishes scholarly articles on the intersection between law and culture. She can be reached at *https://psusanayres.com/*

www.ingramcontent.com/pod-product-compliance
Lightning Source LLC
Chambersburg PA
CBHW022047080426
42734CB00009B/1275